ROBERT SKEEN'S

AUTOBIOGRAPHY.

AUTOBIOGRAPHY

OF

MR. ROBERT SKEEN,

PRINTER.

WRITTEN AT THE SPECIAL REQUEST OF

A BOOKSELLER WHO HAS BENEFITED FOR THIRTY-FOUR YEARS

BY THE UNCEASING AND CHEERFUL ATTENTION TO HIS

OFTEN VERY INTRICATE CATALOGUE WORK,

EXECUTED UNDER MR. ROBERT SKEEN'S SUPERVISION,

AT MR. G. NORMAN'S PRINTING ESTABLISHMENT,

MAIDEN LANE, COVENT GARDEN.

100 *Copies printed at the expense of this obliged and ever grateful friend, by*
MESSRS. WYMAN & SONS, 74–75, GREAT QUEEN STREET,
LINCOLN'S-INN FIELDS, LONDON, W.C.
1876.

AUTOBIOGRAPHY.

I was born on the 9th of October, 1797, in the village of Tweedmouth, in North Durham. My father, *William Skeen*, was a fisherman, whose ancestors had resided near Elgin, in Morayshire, for many generations; but his father, in early life, had left the paternal home in Scotland and migrated to the North of England, where he married, and lived to a good old age. He died in Tweedmouth about the year 1802, highly respected by all who knew him.

My father married *Margaret Nesbit*, the daughter of a neighbouring farmer. They had a family of six sons and four daughters; I was the oldest. To maintain so many was a severe struggle, on the scanty and precarious earnings of a fisherman. But we never suffered actual want.

It was the great desire of our parents to give us as good an education as the village *School.* schools could bestow; and this they accomplished. We were taught reading, writing, and arithmetic. It was a good foundation on

B

which to build. I was blessed with a retentive memory, and could read fluently when only *five* years old. The *Bible* was the great school-book; and the portions I committed to memory (as extra lessons) were considered proofs of unusual ability by the seniors of the village. I was a great favourite among the old fishermen, and frequently joined them when fishing on the sea-shore or at the rocks off the mouth of the Tweed. Some of them predicted that I would become a Doctor of Divinity! Two, indeed, of my village companions attained to that distinction,—the Rev. Dr. Robert Lee, of Edinburgh (whose life was published a few years ago), and the Rev. Dr. Nisbet, many years a missionary in India. Another, though younger companion, was John Wilson, author of the well-known "Tales of the Borders." All the three have been dead several years.

Having a vigorous constitution, I took great delight in all the outdoor games of boyhood, and was especially distinguished for fleetness of foot. More than once I accompanied an uncle in his visits to the Cheviot Hills, which I keenly enjoyed.

But my school-boy days soon came to an end. *Apprenticed.* It was necessary I should work. On the 5th of March, 1810 (when I was not quite 12½ years old), I was ushered into the printing-office of Mr. Lochhead, of Berwick-on-Tweed. He was rather a harsh man; but I liked the business very well, and took to it kindly. Our hours of work were long—from about 6 a.m. to 8 p.m. Notwithstanding, I found time to read at night, often when the rest of the family were asleep. Many of our friends supplied me with books, for my father's shelves were but scantily furnished. He had, however, *Reading.* among others, Josephus's "Wars of the Jews," by L'Estrange, which I read through more than once. An odd volume (the last) of the *Spectator*, also, I remember, highly interested me.

An effort of memory some time after I was apprenticed had nearly changed my whole course of life. I had heard a sermon one *Memory.* day from a reverend gentleman who lived some miles off, on the words of Paul, "God forbid that I should glory, save in the Cross of the Lord Jesus Christ." It was a forcible and well-delivered discourse. Some twelve months afterwards he came on a visit to Berwick, and there preached the same sermon. I remembered it all, and, going home, wrote it down from beginning to end. The manuscript was handed about; my friends were not a little proud of it; and some gentlemen in the neighbourhood into whose hands it fell talked seriously of sending me to *college*. But I felt no special inclination to study theology, and eventually preferred to remain a Printer rather than to become a Parson. This I have never regretted.

In the Printing-office I learned to work at press as well as at case. The latter, of course, was more congenial; and the master soon discovered that to him it was more profitable. Our work consisted chiefly in bringing out editions of popular works, which were sold in numbers or parts (6d. or 1s. each) by agents (*colporteurs*), who carried them through the towns and villages in the South of Scotland and North of England. Others beside my master were engaged in a similar business. In this way, thousands of copies of the Bible (usually 4to. with notes), Brown's Dictionary, the "General Gazetteer," &c., were circulated among the poorer classes, who could spend a shilling or sixpence for a monthly part, but never would have saved enough to buy the whole book at once.

Printing-office.

There were in the office five or six boys and two or three journeymen. Among the boys a spirit of emulation arose, a strife who should compose the greatest number of lines in a given time. This lasted for weeks, or rather months. We put ourselves on our mettle, and worked as if life and death depended on the issue. It was for the barren honour of victory. Our extraordinary efforts added not a penny to our stipulated wages. The master was the sole gainer.—No! we also were gainers. At least, I know that the impulse then given, and the singular swiftness and accuracy in composing

Rivalry.

which I then acquired, never left me, and proved of great advantage in my future career.

We had very few holidays. It was not the fashion to give them, and therefore they were not expected. I had formed acquaintance with a few young men, who were bent on self-improvement:* so we met on stated evenings, and spent a few hours in reading and discussion. These meetings attracted the attention of several of our seniors, who joined and encouraged us. They proved very profitable, not only by the useful knowledge we acquired, but by the habit then induced of expressing our thoughts with great readiness and accuracy.

Mutual improvement.

About the same time, also, at the request of a few gentlemen interested in the education of the young, I undertook, in conjunction with another, the management of a Sunday-school in an adjoining village (Ord).

Sunday-school.

On the expiration of my apprenticeship I went

* One of my friends had been a *shepherd* in his earlier life among the Cheviot Hills. He and other herds formed a *circulating library.* The sheep-walks were very extensive, and in some places there were boundaries of loose stone walls. In certain crannies in these walls they agreed to deposit whatever books they might acquire—having first read them. The next who passed that way took the volume so deposited, leaving another in its place. The first, after being read, was carried miles farther on, and left in another similar depository; and so on, for a *circuit* of thirty or forty miles. The shepherds seldom saw each other, but their books bound them together,—profitably occupying their leisure time, and expanding their intellect.

Edinburgh. to Edinburgh; visited several relatives there; and, after a few days, finding no employment, walked westward forty miles to Glasgow. In this city I first heard the celebrated *Dr. Chalmers.* He preached *Glasgow.* in his own church, from the text: " In the world ye shall have tribulation; but be of good cheer; I have overcome the world." The place was crowded. I stood the whole time. Though he *read* the sermon, I have never witnessed such breathless attention in any audience during my whole life.

I was much pleased with Glasgow; visited the University, the Cathedral (see "Rob Roy"), and other public buildings. It has wonderfully increased since that time. There being no prospect of *Canal.* employment here, I left Glasgow by the way of the Stirling Canal;—it was very pleasant travelling in the canal boats, though rather slow, especially in passing through the locks; I think at one place there were seventeen in succession. On reaching Edinburgh I stayed a few days, and visited most of the interesting localities in the city and neighbourhood. It was now needful I should return home, and I walked from Edinburgh to Berwick, fifty miles, in one day !

Instead of proceeding at once to London, my *At home.* father persuaded me to engage in the salmon-fishing with him, as extra hands were wanted from May to October. It was to me

a very pleasant season.   Salmon were abundant.
I had a good deal of leisure time, for we could
only fish at certain periods of the tide,
the sea driving us twice a day from our   *Fisher-*
fishing-ground, which was a sand-bank   *men.*
at the mouth of the river.   As the tides varied, so
did our hours of work.   We were often up at three
and four in the morning—often late at night.
The *weather* was of no consequence—hot or cold,
sunshine or storm, wet or dry—it was all the same
to us.   Sometimes, on a hot day, while waiting for
the signal from the boatman at the " Stell," I
have gone to sleep on the sandy beach, and, on
waking, found I had been drenched to the skin
by a sudden shower. It did me no harm. Fishermen very rarely catch cold on the sea-shore. This
sort of education, no doubt, hardened and invi-
gorated the body.   But the mind, also, received
some education during my fisherman-life.   I had
a desire to learn *Greek,* and induced the
schoolmaster of the village to join me.   *Greek.*
We found a neighbouring clergyman (Rev. W.
Whitehouse) willing to give us lessons. We procured grammars and lexicons, and went doggedly
to work.   Often the grammar accompanied me to
the sea-shore, where the fishermen, notwithstanding the novelty of the affair, encouraged rather
than hindered me ; for, though unlearned, they
were by no means ignorant men.

The fishing season came to an end before I had

caught a thorough knowledge of Greek. But what I then learnt has proved very serviceable during the whole of my life, and forms a pleasing reminiscence of my fishing days.

It was now decided I should go to London; so, in November, 1817, I took a passage in the Berwick smack *Ceres*, Captain W. Crow. We had a pleasant voyage of five days. Off Aldborough, I remember, we heard the bells tolling at midnight for the funeral of the lamented Princess Charlotte of Wales.

Reach London.

My departure made the first gap in our family circle. Of my five brothers, one died young, another went to sea, and, to our great grief, was drowned in the Baltic; a third, *Alexander*, was a printer, and latterly carried on business in Great St. Helen's, Bishopsgate; he died suddenly at Ventnor, in 1873. His business is conducted by one of his nephews. In the same year my youngest brother, *William*, died on his sixty-first birthday. He had devoted himself to reporting for the Press, first for the *Edinburgh Courant*. He afterwards came to London, and for several years reported for the *Standard*. In the gallery of the House of Commons he was well known and highly esteemed. Besides reporting, he contributed many original articles to various magazines. My second brother and our four sisters still survive.

Brothers.

With such a family, it will be readily understood that my parents, when I left the " hearth-stone," could bestow on me little beside their blessing. That was enough. My heart was high with hope, and I could never forget their bright example of faith and fortitude.

On arriving in London I was kindly received by two relatives. But the letters of introduction I carried helped me to no employment. For a month I went about inquiring, and then thought of entering the Company's service and going to the East Indies. But soon afterwards I obtained work at Camberwell, where the *Encyclo-pædia Metropolitana* was then being *Get work.* printed. Never since have I been unemployed.

I remained at Camberwell for a considerable period, and, having saved a few pounds, resolved to take a *wife*. That was a *Marry.* step in the right direction, and never have 1 repented taking it ! For my wife has proved one of the choice ones of the earth. Never man had a better. We were both under twenty-two years of age when married on July 3, 1819 ; and now, after nearly fifty-seven years, my dear partner still retains all the cheerfulness and much of the activity of her early life. On our *Golden Wed-ding,* in 1869, many kind friends united with the family in its celebration.

When the Printing-office at Camberwell was closed, towards the end of 1819, the overseer, who had proved very friendly, recommended me to take charge of a small office at Guildford, in Surrey. I accordingly went thither; but after a few weeks I found there was scarcely any business doing, and little prospect of an increase; so I resigned and returned to London, and got employment at Messrs. Gilbert's, in St. John's Square. After a while the work there became slack. As I could not afford to be idle, I left and went to Mr. *Dove's*, also in St. John's Square. Here there was abundance of work, and I did very well.

Mr. Norman was then an apprentice in the office, and we became acquainted. An accident introduced me to the *Reading Room ;* for, during a pressure of business, Mr. Dove asked me one evening to take some proof-sheets home to read. I gladly consented, and finished them before I slept. On presenting them in the morning, he could scarcely believe I had gone through them. On examination, however, he was satisfied in all respects. Thenceforth I was installed as a *Reader*, and continued in that capacity for some years. On the retirement of our excellent and worthy overseer, *Mr. B. Clark,** I was appointed in his place. This situation I found was no sinecure; for the office, was large and the master had a peculiar temper. However, on the whole, I had no great reason to complain.

* Author of the well-known hymn, "Not lost, but gone before."

In 1832 he retired from business, chiefly, as was understood, in consequence of the death of Sir William Middleton, who had supplied him with money to carry on the business, and was a partner in it. The young baronet insisted on a dissolution of the partnership. This was done. Everything was sold off; and Dove, having no family, retired to a village in Suffolk, where he died a few years ago, at the age of 75. He had greatly coveted civic honours, and offered himself a candidate for the Aldermanship of Bishopsgate Without, and afterwards made efforts to obtain the office of Sheriff, but, in each case, he was disappointed.

When the art of stereotyping was first discovered, Dove took great interest in it, and built a foundry on his premises, for the casting of his own plates. Many visitors called to see the process, to the no small emolument of the stereotyper.

I had not been long engaged as *Reader* when Dove employed me in compiling *Indexes* to many of the works he printed. This I did at night, when the day's work was over, for which I received extra pay. I also wrote for him several *Prefaces, Memoirs*, &c., especially in 1827 and 1828, when he printed and published, in thirty volumes, " *The British Essayists*, with Prefaces, &c., by the Rev. R. Lynam, A.M., and others."—I believe I was the only " *others*." Soon afterwards I was employed in editing a new edition of "*Joe Miller*," in which I omitted all the coarse jests, and inserted a large number of attic anecdotes. I remember. also, in reprinting Barbauld's *Evenings at Home*,* two tales were found to be copyright, and my pen had to furnish two *original* tales, but with the same titles. One was " The Council of Quadrupeds."

Before Dove's Printing-office was finally closed I had three distinct offers of employment from different printers. Several kind friends also urged me to commence business on my own account ; to this, however, as I had no money, I would not consent. I preferred the offer made by *Mr. Norman*. It was not the most brilliant, so far as remuneration was concerned, but *mere money* was never my chief object. I had become acquainted with Mr. Norman several years before, and knew that I should find in him a congenial spirit—one with whom I could feel at home, and whose kindness and liberality I might safely trust. Nor have I been disappointed :—for, during the forty-four years we have been together, I have never had any reason to regret my position.

But, indeed, in the whole affair I was acting in the spirit of an admonition which had been impressed upon me in early life :—" Trust in the

* If I recollect rightly, this was one of a series, in 32mo, known as "*Dove's Classics.*"

Lord with all thine heart, and lean not unto thine own understanding ; in all thy ways acknowledge Him, and He shall direct thy paths." So with this conviction I entered on my duties in the Printing-office, carrying out my old motto : " Whatsoever thy hand findeth to do, do it with thy might." I can truly say that *work* never was a burden to me. I enjoyed it.

Mr. Norman's business steadily increased, which was a source of pleasure to me. For his industry, punctuality, and unswerving integrity deserved success ; besides, it gave the greater occupation to my faculties.

Shortly after our marriage, in 1819, my wife and I joined the Church of the United Brethren (or Moravians). This Church *Moravians.* originated in Bohemia (in 1457), 42 years after the martyrdom of John Huss. Indeed, the Brethren have been called " Bohemian Hussites." In a few years they increased and multiplied, and had many congregations in Poland, as well as in Bohemia and Moravia. They were the first who translated and printed the Bible in their own language. But in 1510 a furious persecution arose, and they were scattered to the four winds. Indeed, their Papal enemies believed that the " pestilent heresy " had been completely extirpated. For, in reference to them, in the Lateran Council of 1513, it was declared : " There is an end of resistance to the Papal rule and religion, opposers there exist no more." But a few were left in Moravia, who transmitted their principles to their descendants. Very little was known of them, however, until about the year 1720, when some of them emigrated into Saxony, where they found a home and liberty of conscience on the estate of Count Zinzendorf. Congregations were

Missions. soon afterwards formed in various parts of Germany, in Holland, and in England, and also in America. They have been distinguished by efforts for the conversion and civilization of the Heathen—among the *Negroes* in the West Indies and Surinam—the American *Indians* —the *Greenlanders* and *Eskimoes*—the *Hottentots* and *Caffres*—the *Mongolians* and *Australians*, &c. The translation of the Bible into the native languages has ever been kept steadily in view.

The only congregation of the Moravians in London is in Fetter Lane. It was never numerous. But I found myself at home, aud took a lively interest in the affairs of the Church at large. There were in the congregation some largehearted and intellectual men; and meetings with such were organized and maintained for several years. Our readings and conversation were equally pleasant and profitable. Among them were Mr. Benham, late of Regent Square, a great book-collector, author of many pamphlets and compiler of several larger works; Dr. Horsfield, Librarian of the East-India House, a botanist long

resident in Java, who discovered the real proper-
ties of the Upas-tree ; Rev. P. La Trobe, secre-
tary to the Missions of the Brethren, &c. These
and others are all gone—I alone am left !

In 1835 I was appointed the " Steward " * of
the congregation. My duties were multifarious,
involving the receipt of all contributions and
payment of all expenses, and the providing of all
things necessary for the order and maintenance
of the various services. All this occupied a considerable portion of my leisure time at night. It
was truly a labour of love, for in the spirit of the
Church such services are performed gratuitously.
I held the stewardship for 35 years, and in 1871
resigned it (being in my 74th year) to a younger
and more active member of the congregation.

I was also elected to represent the congregation
at Provincial Synods on three several occasions.
These are held at intervals of six or eight years,
and choose the Board of Direction, revise the
constitution of the Church, &c.

In 1853 I was chosen a member of the Society
for the Furtherance of the Gospel, which office I
hold to the present day. The Society's chief
object (beside " furthering " missionaries of the
Brethren's Church who pass through London), is
the maintenance of the mission among the Eski-

* Previously I had been a member of the Committee, and
remain so to the present day.

moes on the coast of Labrador. For this purpose they have a ship of their own, which has, for above 100 years, successfully performed the voyage to and from that dreary and dangerous coast. One of the Labrador missionaries, Mr. Miertsching,* accompanied Captain M'Clure as interpreter, in the "Investigator," when they discovered the North-west Passage (Oct. 26, 1850).

About the year 1835 an extraordinary and unsought-for offer of £1,000 was made to me, by two kind friends, to enable me to go into business on my own account, the money to be repaid when convenient; and if I should fail, the loss to be entirely theirs. Their only object was "to enable me, by an increase of means, to increase my ability to do good; and also to keep the boys about me." (Our family was rapidly increasing.) Mr. Ridgway (the grandfather of the present), bookseller, in Piccadilly, was also favourable to the project, and promised his support. My friends, generally, pressed me to accept the generous offer. But I hesitated, and sought counsel. I shrunk from the responsibility of bearing such a burden of debt, and felt that the cares and anxieties of business thus burdened would not suit my temperament. I therefore, with grateful thanks, declined the offer of my kind friends.

* He was a Vend, born in Upper Lusatia. In 1875 he died at Kleinwelka, in Saxony, aged 58 years.

Having mentioned the matter to Mr. Norman, he at once proposed to increase my salary, with promises of collateral and prospective advantages (such as taking the boys apprentice, &c.), all of which he kindly and generously carried out. At the same time he suggested that I should insure my life, which I immediately did.

Of our *eight* sons—one died in early life—the remaining *seven* were all in due time apprenticed to Mr. Norman. We had also *four* daughters—two of whom died in childhood.

In 1836, having been absent from home above eighteen years, I was enabled to carry out a long-cherished desire to visit the " old familiar haunts." It will readily be imagined that an uninterrupted corre-spondence was maintained with my be-loved relatives. Moreover, I had had the pleasure of welcoming my parents to my home in London on more than one occasion. My dear wife, with two of the children, had also visited them in Tweedmouth a few years before. *Home-ward Ho !*

I embarked on July 27, on board the steamer *Water-witch*. (There was no railway to the North in those days.) In the Hum-ber we got on board the *Eclipse*, for Newcastle ; thence we proceeded by the *Ardincaple*, bound for Leith. But in Berwick Bay we encountered a violent storm. I shall never forget the scene—it really was grand. Billow after *Voyage. Storm.*

billow rose high above the vessel's bows, threatening to swallow us up ; while the ship, persistently surmounting every crest, seemed to defy their fury. We were obliged, however, to turn back and take refuge behind the Farne Islands. Next day we endeavoured to reach the Firth of Forth, but could not, and were compelled to run for Berwick Harbour. Here several of the passengers landed. This was rather an advantage to me, for now I was *at home.* I had, however, a narrow escape. On stepping from the paddle-box to the pier I should have fallen into the sea if a sailor had not caught my arm—and saved my life !

Narrow escape.

My thus unexpected arrival gave great joy to all my friends, especially to my parents. Since I had left the village many of my acquaintances had died, or gone to other places ; several of the old fishermen, however, remained, and were glad to see me—the more so, as some remarked that I still retained many of my old habits, and had not forgotten the Northumbrian dialect.

At home.

I paid a visit, among many others, to the clergyman who had given me lessons in Greek. He was very cordial. Brought out a MS. volume of poetry (I believe he had not fixed on a title), and insisted on reading to me a few pages. He wanted my opinion of its merits. So I proposed to glance over it—which I did very rapidly.

"Well—what did I think?"—"I can't find any bones in it."—"Bones! Mr. Skeen; what do you mean?"—"Why, murders, bloody battles!" —"Well," he replied, "you will find one allusion to a battle!"—Two lines I remember:

"While Roger whistled at the plough,
And Nancy milk'd the nut-brown cow"—

may be taken as a fair sample of the whole. It seemed to me somewhat in the style of Beattie's "*Minstrel*." But the good man wanted to print it—by subscription. His chief anxiety, however, was about the *pointing*. I advised him to leave that to the printers, who understood punctuation better than most authors. This he evidently doubted. The precious volume had occupied much of his time during several years—to the exclusion, I fear, of many more weighty matters. In fact, it seemed to have both narrowed and enfeebled his intellect. What became of his poetry I never learnt. Our interview had a curious termination. I had noticed that he asked me, as I thought, several irrelevant questions and made remarks I did not quite understand. As I was about to take leave, he made an observation which suddenly enlightened me, and I said: "Mr. Whitehouse, do you know to whom you are speaking?"—"Yes; to *William* Skeen, to be sure!" —"Well, I thought so; but I am not William." —"Not William! Surely you cannot be *Robert?*"

—"I am, though," was my rejoinder—to his great joy and amazement. The likeness between us, in early life, was rather striking. We had not seen each other for above eighteen years; but my old friend had seen him recently, and was struck with the resemblance. My brother was then reporting for the *Courant*, at Edinburgh, where I hoped in a few days to have the pleasure of meeting him.

I visited Mr. Whitehouse more than once, enjoying his conversation while strolling along the sea-shore. Nor did we omit a plunge in the deep. But my time was limited. After six days of pleasant intercourse with my friends, and visiting most of my old haunts, I took leave of my revered parents, and started for Edinburgh by coach. At Cockburnspath (Coppersmith) (where Cromwell found himself in a difficulty, before the battle of Dunbar) the horses became restive, and we were nearly upset. At Edinburgh I was joyfully welcomed by my brother William. He also was married, and had a family. We spent two or three days happily together.

On taking leave of him at Leith, I embarked in the steamer *Pegasus*, about to start for Hull. There was a large number of passengers. All went well till we passed the Farne Islands (where Grace Darling and her father so heroically rescued the shipwrecked crew of the *Forfarshire*). I was chatting on deck with some of the passengers, when the ship struck with great force:—some were capsized—all staggered. I looked to the shore, and calculated we should be able to swim to land. Presently the carpenter reported five feet water in the hold. We had struck a rock *under water*. It was not marked in the chart—but there are many such on that coast—and the captain ought to have kept farther out. His silly excuse was that he wished the passengers to have a good view of the picturesque and precipitous shores of Northumberland! We discovered that he was a novice and a relative of the owners.

A signal of distress being hoisted, a fishing-boat came alongside. Her master undertook to run our vessel on shore, between two ledges of rock, which he skilfully accomplished. On landing we found ourselves at the small village of Newton-by-the-Sea.

The ship's bows had been completely cut through by the sharp edge of the rock. The captain started at once for Edinburgh, to apprise the owners of his mishap. He soon returned with several carpenters, and within twenty-four hours afterwards the *Pegasus* was reported seaworthy. In the meantime, several of us had strolled about the adjoining country. We were about two miles north of the picturesque ruin of Dunstanboro' Castle, which stands on a promontory jutting into the sea. Some of our fellow-passengers, however, had been thoroughly frightened, and refused to embark, preferring a journey by land to any further exposure to the dangers of the deep.

The *Pegasus*, however, got to Hull safely. I had written to London, from Newton, to allay anxiety, which would naturally arise on account of our detention. But the postal service was very defective in that fishing village, and I got to London before the letter, having embarked in the *Vivid* at Hull.

I found all the family well, and the business in the office going on smoothly. The excursion had done me good, and I resumed work with renewed vigour.

In 1838 I again visited the Tweed. On that occasion, accompanied by my dear father, I made a pilgrimage to *Lindisfarne*, the celebrated *Holy Island*. A flat sand, about two miles wide, separates it from the coast of Northumberland during low water; but when the tide rises, the sand is overflowed, and Lindisfarne is then truly an island. Many have been drowned in attempting to cross when the tide was rising.

We got over safely, but barefooted; for the sand is in many places not merely wet, but full of shallow pools, which must be crossed. There are small heaps of stones and poles at intervals, to mark the way for travellers across the sands.

The island is highly interesting, locally and historically; of course there are legends also.

The *Cathedral* is a grand ruin. There are remains also of the old *Monastery*.

St. Cuthbert is the patron saint, not of Holy Island only, but of all Northumbria. His body, after many adventures, now rests in Durham Cathedral. The Danes had ravaged the island more than once. There is a fine stone cross in the centre of its only village. I made rather copious notes of this visit, which were afterwards expanded and preserved in a " luminous, learned, and lengthy Log."

A few days afterwards (Sept. 4), with two of my nephews, I made a journey to Norham Castle, and St. Cuthbert's Chapel at the junction of the Till and the Tweed. It proved a very wet day, but our spirits were not damped. In Norham churchyard I visited the grave of my maternal grandmother, and copied the inscription on her tombstone. The vicar, the Rev. Dr. Gilly, author of the Life of *Felix Neff*, was from home, but his son courteously showed us his beautiful garden, which had been laid out by the sculptor *Chantrey*. The square tower of Norham Castle is still in a fair state of preservation : it is about 100 feet high. In and around it are occasionally dug up relics of antiquity. In the village is a fine old stone cross.

At that time there was no bridge over the Tweed at Norham, so we crossed to the north side by the ferry-boat at Upsettlington, a little above

Ladykirk, the seat of W. Robertson, Esq. Our walk on the Scottish side of the river was delightful. On arriving opposite the mouth of the *Till*, we procured a boat, and pulled across to St. Cuthbert's Chapel. The present structure had been built on the site of the ancient one ; but though comparatively modern, it was sadly dilapidated. Doors and windows were gone, the ceiling nearly destroyed, and the floor strewed with rubbish. But where was the cele-

No boat.   brated *Stone Boat ?* We had been told at the village on the Scotch side of the river that we should find it—cracked, indeed, but still entire. Some years before, it had been converted into a swine's trough by the farmer of the land on which the Chapel stands ; now, not a vestige of it was to be seen. Thinking it might have been broken in pieces, I picked up what I hoped was a fragment, and returned to our boat much disappointed.

On landing, we resolved to walk home by the

Flodden.   English side of the Tweed. We were here not far distant from *Flodden Field* (which I had seen in early life), where was fought the famous battle described by Scott with a pen of fire in the marvellous pages of " *Marmion*."

Close by us was *Twizell Castle*, begun by a Sir Francis Blake many years before, but never finished, and now actually decaying. Soon afterwards we met an old shepherd, to whom I told the tale of our disappointment, and showed him what I supposed to be a piece of the Boat. " No, no," he said, " the *Boat* was *red* sandstone." (Mine was *grey*.) " But what has become of the Boat ? " " I know," he replied ; " the former tenant turned it into a swine's trough, and the pigs cracked it. He never prospered after ; lost his leg, and is now herding sheep over yonder. The present farmer broke it in pieces, and used them for draining-tiles in the field where the Chapel stands. This was about three years since. I saw it done, for I was herding there at the time." I told him it was downright sacrilege. The old herd thought so too, and added that " heavy misfortunes had fallen on his family." I felt half inclined to go back and dig up the drain !

But, after all, that was not the end of the famous *Stone Boat*, in which St. Cuthbert had floated down the Tweed from Melrose Abbey, 1,200 years ago.

A day or two afterwards I was invited to a " *kettle*," by some of my old friends, the fishermen. To them I related the story of my pilgrimage to St. Cuthbert's Chapel. Old Swinhoe, one of our party (once an active smuggler, shrewd and intelligent), took up the story, and told me that when Sir Francis Blake learnt the fate of the Boat he " waxed exceeding wroth," and commanded the sacrilegious farmer instantly to dig up the precious fragments, and convey them to

E

Twizell House, his seat on the banks of the Till. There they remain. Swinhoe, seeing the interest I took in the old Stone Boat, said one of his nephews was living with Sir Francis, and much in his confidence, and he would send to him for a *bit*. I thanked him, but thought no more of it. However, on the morning I was preparing to leave for London, Swinhoe appeared with a *bit of the boat*, nearly as large as my hand, rather rounded, as if broken off between the bottom and the side. I carried it home as a singular relic of antiquity.

There is an interesting account of St. Cuthbert and his Boat in *Ridpath's Border History* (I believe now a scarce 4to volume). It is there stated that the then Sir Francis Blake (100 years ago), with a party of his friends launched the Stone Boat on the river, where it floated with a man on board; thus proving, so far, the truth of the old legend. In *Chambers' Journal*, a few years since, I read an article on the *Boat*, but the writer was evidently ignorant of its later history; indeed, I believe not many persons are acquainted with the particulars which came to my knowledge during this visit to the Tweed.

On returning home I resumed with fresh zest my onerous duties in the Printing-office, as Overseer and Reader. Not contented with these, I undertook the editing of a new edition of *Loskiel's* History of the Mission

Loskiel.

among the *North American Indians.* It had been
originally published in German, then translated
into English, and was now out of print. This
was more than a new edition, for the original had
ended with the year 1787, and I continued the
History to 1838, besides adding much additional
information and copious notes to the old narra-
tive; considerably expanding, also, the " Prelimi-
nary Account of the Indians."

This involved much laborious research, and
occupied many of my leisure hours; or
rather many hours which I ought to   *Sleep.*
have devoted to sleep. But I cannot say that
I ever suffered by curtailing the hours of sleep.
It appears to me that when mind and body are
fatigued by labour, sleep follows closely on rest,
—it is sounder and more *satisfying ;* therefore
less of it is required for refreshment and reno-
vation.

However, I never suffered any avocations or
engagements to interfere with my duty in the
Printing-office. That was a trust on no account
to be neglected; and I am not aware
that the work ever fell into arrears when   *Work.*
human effort could avert it. But to me was given
by the Almighty a large measure of health and
strength; and such was the kind consideration
of Mr. Norman, that to work for him and with
him was a real pleasure. Only once was I prostrated and rendered feeble as a child by *influ-*

enza ; but in a few weeks I rallied, and, as the physician predicted, and I may thankfully acknowledge, became stronger than ever.

Very few outside of a printing-office can form a proper conception of the wear-and-tear involved in the management of the business. And the pressure seems to increase year by year. There is not sufficient time allowed to get through the work with any degree of comfort. I remember when steam and railways began to play their wonderful part in aiding and even superseding manual labour, it was confidently assumed that man's burdens would be lightened and his anxieties lessened. But the contrary has proved the fact. All manner of work is now required to be performed at a railroad pace. This is especially found to be the case in a printing-office ; and an overseer's duties and responsibilities are consequently increased. He must meet the demands of authors and publishers at all hazards—sometimes in an emergency with the extra help of imperfectly-trained assistants, who may be sadly deficient in the virtues of *punctuality* and *promptitude*—often by extending the working hours until late at night, or even all night long. Calculating the time each work will occupy, with the means at his disposal, and so stimulating accordingly that which is most urgent, while still solicitous about that which he may be compelled for a time to leave to the ordinary routine. But with all our pressure, Mr. Norman never would permit any work on Sunday; and he was right—I never could learn that *Sunday work* was an advantage. The men who worked seven days a week, as a rule, earned no more than those who rested on the seventh—Monday, with the former, was usually a "*saint's day.*"

But a great drawback to the progress of work, especially in cases of urgency, is the almost *illegible handwriting* of many authors. The loss of time and of patience it occasions is incalculable. No compensation for the "bad copy" really compensates the compositor. Of course, in this case, an intelligent workman possesses a vast advantage over his more ignorant companion. But it is to all a great evil. Often have I, when pamphlets were urgent, transcribed page after page of the *illegible stuff* for the compositor, in order to save time in forwarding the proof-sheets and diminish expense in correcting them.

Indeed, cases have occurred where the MS. has been returned to the author because his writing could not be read. Not long ago, a whole volume was thus sent back to be re-written, which I believe to be no solitary instance. Were manuscripts carefully prepared before they are sent to the printer, a great saving would be effected both in time and expense. That always unsatisfactory item, "*corrections,*" in a printer's bill, would be considerably reduced, and the feelings of authors and publishers no longer irritated by the supposed unreasonableness of the charge. For the corrections of a sheet sometimes cost more than its composition.

I had early experience in the difficulties of " *bad copy*." While yet an apprentice, I was put on a work which required great patience and thoughtfulness to decipher the manuscript. My usual practice was, when I got a " taking," to sit down under my frame, and carefully ponder over it. A half-hour or so thus occupied I found to be a saving of time. I had mastered the hieroglyphics, and went on composing without interruption.

Some remarkable cases of " *illegibility* " have come before me. The late *Lord Brougham* wrote an " abominable fist." So uncouth and Caliban-like were the marks that did duty for words, that ever and anon the compositor might exclaim— " What have we here, a man or a fish ? " Another well-known author and popular preacher, still living, has in like manner often tried our patience. How should I have rejoiced if my pen had possessed the power of Ithuriel's spear, and by a touch made the *reptile-looking scrawl* start into proper shape ! The late *Mr. Lilly*, the book-seller, wrote a strange, bold hand. The copy of his catalogues was a sad puzzle to the uninitiated. Mr. Norman usually printed for him. On one occasion, however, he took the copy of a catalogue to a neighbouring printing-office. But almost immediately the manuscript was returned to him, with the remark that the compositors could not read it. "Not read it!" he cried; "why, they never complain of it at Norman's!" This was very true. We had got used to the infliction; and our compositors had ceased to grumble, because they received extra compensation for his "*extra bad copy.*"

In 1842, my third son, *Robert*, went to New Zealand in his 18th year. He had been apprenticed to Mr. Norman; but his *Robert.* eyesight failing, it was thought advisable he should leave the office. A friend offered to make him a sailor. He went a few coasting voyages; but his course was soon changed. A company had been formed for the purpose of manufacturing the *New Zealand flax* into cordage, &c.; and my son was chosen by the manager (Mr. Terry) to accompany him to the colony. Robert got married the day before they sailed. He had a good outfit and a prosperous voyage. Operations were commenced in the bush; but they did not succeed. From want of skill or steadiness, or an unexpected torrent which damaged their *New Zealand* machinery, the whole affair in a few *adventure.* months came to an end. Those employed in it were left almost destitute and without remuneration, and had to struggle for existence as best they could. My son has had a large

32

experience of colonial life, and his occupations have been strangely varied. At one time he was *Postman.* *postman,* his *beat* extending above 170 miles, from Auckland to the opposite coast, and along the western shore of the northern island. Part of his journey lay through woods— a pig-track being the only road—rivers he had to cross in native canoes. Another portion consisted of thirty miles of loose sandy beach. But he was stout and cheerful. A more congenial occupation *Printer.* was his employment on the " *New Zealander* "; and after that he was engaged in the printing of the *Bible* in the *Maori* language, which he had the honour of completing. When that was at an end, he took a farm, and was doing *Burnt out.* well, when one morning, during his temporary absence, the *bark* house in which he lived caught fire, and was burnt to the ground. Everything was consumed, his poor wife and four little children barely escaping with life. Worse than all, the shock to his wife brought on an illness which carried her off in a few weeks. He gave up the farm, and turned again to the printing. In 1857 he married a second wife. *Land-holder.* Soon afterwards he obtained a grant of 150 acres of land at Mangawai; nearly all of it was *forest*, mostly noble gum-trees. He began to clear and cultivate; was made a justice of the peace, and might have established himself as a great *chief!* Unfortunately, however, he was elected Member of the Colonial Parliament. This involved attendance at Auckland, and the farming at Mangawai was neglected. *An M.P.* His land was eventually sold, and he returned to the capital with his family. He is now employed as agent, collector of news, &c. for the papers in the Thames district, on the opposite side of the harbour, where the gold-fields lately attracted a large population.

In 1846 I was summoned to the funeral of my beloved mother. She had attained the age of 72 years. There were then four of her sons living in London. None of us had forgotten the *Fifth Commandment*, and we honoured our parents accordingly. But when our venerable father had reached threescore and ten, it was suggested by my thoughtful wife that he ought to *rest* from his labours—(few men ever laboured more incessantly)—and that a fund should be formed to maintain our parents in comfort so long as they lived. This was promptly and cheerfully carried into execution. No one of us felt the duty to be a burden—its performance, I believe, was found to be a blessing.

On the news of our dear mother's death, the four sons started for Berwick; but the railway was only completed to Newcastle—sixty miles farther we travelled by stage. At Alnehead, a village among the Cheviots, we stopped for refreshment, and in descending from the coach I fell, and a bottle

F

in my pocket was broken into shivers under me, but I rose *unhurt!* We travelled all night, and arrived at home in the early dawn. The funeral was numerously attended by relatives and sympathizing friends.

Our time was limited, but before returning we visited *Loanend*, a few miles up the Tweed, the birthplace of our departed mother, and *Horncliff*, another village, a little higher, where some of the family resided. Not far from these is the *Chain Bridge*, connecting England and Scotland. It is the first of the kind ever erected in Great Britain, and is much admired. It was built by Captain Brown, who afterwards constructed the chain pier at Brighton.

Excursions.
In the following year Mrs. Skeen and I were again at Tweedmouth. We returned home by the railway (now finished) to York, visiting its grand old Minster, with the noble and beautifully-ornamented Chapter House. Thence we proceeded to Leeds, Bradford, Manchester, and other towns on our way to London.

Henceforward, indeed, taking an annual holiday of a fortnight in summer, we made successive trips to various localities, visiting most of the principal towns in England, and nearly all the watering-places on the South Coast. The beautiful *Isle of Wight* was a favourite resort. Of our first visit to the island I have preserved a long, circumstantial, and illustrated account. On one occasion, with two of my sons, I rambled to *Stonehenge*, thence to *Salisbury*, and through the *New Forest*, where I copied the inscription on the stone which marks the spot where King *William Rufus* was slain. In the adjoining village of Minstead we found one *Purkess*, a shoemaker, who is probably a descendant of the peasant that conveyed the body of the King from the Forest to Winchester in his cart.

Canterbury we visited more than once. With my son Alexander, on one occasion, I attended the old French service in the Walloon Chapel in the crypt of the Cathedral. We afterwards made an adventurous journey from Canterbury to Deal (18 miles): having started too late, we lost our way in the dark, and risked our lives in crossing the ditches.

In 1856 Mrs. Skeen and I visited *France* in the company of our youngest daughter *Annie*. She had been in *Germany* for several years—first at Ebersdorf, in Saxony, and afterwards in the family of Prince Fürstenberg (whose palace, Donaueschingen, stands at the sources of the Danube). It was said of her, "She speaks German like a native." She had paid us a visit, and was now returning. We parted with her at *Paris*.

Paris.

Of course we enjoyed our trip; but I was not much impressed by the French capital, where we visited most of the principal buildings.

Our daughter a few years afterwards returned home, and is now very happily married to a man after my own heart.

Our eldest daughter (*Justina*) had gone to Germany in 1848, as governess to the children (three sons) of *Prince Reuss*. He was the son of my kind and venerable friend Count Reuss (Henry LV.), who had resided in London many years. On the sudden death of Prince Reuss, his establishment was broken up, and my daughter joined the family of *Count Dohna*, at Lauck, near Mühlhausen, in E. Prussia. In 1858 she came home, and went to Ceylon, where she was married to G. Charter, Esq. He died, after a short illness, in 1866, and she, soon after, took shipping for England with five orphan children. But a violent storm disabled the vessel, which was compelled to take *Long voyage.* refuge in Simon's Bay, Cape of Good Hope; and it was not till after the lapse of 254 days that my beloved daughter and her orphans reached the Thames. She had endured much hardship and anxiety, and lost a large portion of her luggage. A cold, settling on her lungs, carried her off in the 43rd year of her age.

It may be imagined that so many members of the family residing at a distance from *Letter writing.* home (my son William being also in Ceylon at this time), entailed on me a large amount of correspondence. This I never suffered to fall into arrear, feeling that if I did it would inevitably weaken the family bond which so strongly united us together. To answer their letters was to me no trouble; to them it was a source of great pleasure.

Though the business of the office steadily increased, and it became necessary to enlarge the premises, I still found time to discharge the various ecclesiastical duties to which I have already referred; and on the establishment of a *Moravian Magazine*, in 1853, I contributed several papers during successive years, which have always been favourably received. Besides, I was often solicited to write *Birthday Odes, Wedding Lines, Christmas Verses, Jubilee Hymns*, &c., some of which were printed; of most of them copies are preserved.

In 1853, also, I was persuaded to deliver a series of *Twenty-three Lectures* on the Book of Revelation. This originated in *Lectures.* the correspondence with my son William in Ceylon. His letters, containing remarks on some of my views, fell into the hands of a gentleman who took a deep interest in the subject, and who insisted on the duty of publicly lecturing on Prophecy. He procured the use of the chapel. So I consented to deliver a lecture *once a fortnight*. I had nothing prepared, except a few detached notes. Therefore, when I had delivered the *first* lecture, I had to collect and arrange materials,

and write out the *second*, and so on, each fortnight, through the whole series. My early multifarious reading now proved of the greatest service.
It was, no doubt, rather hard work, but I never
failed, often indeed committing large portions of
the lectures to memory as I wrote them down.

I believe it was a benefit, rather than otherwise,
to have the mind steadily intent on business
while in the office—so that the return to study in
the silent hours of night was a refreshment rather
than a weariness.

The Lectures were much approved by those
who heard them. But I had not contemplated
their publication. My son, however—to whom I
transmitted the manuscript as each Lecture was
delivered—besought me to allow him to print them
at the Government Press in Ceylon. The Governor
gave him permission—I could do no less. They
were accordingly printed, and copies sent to
England in 1856. The work was reviewed and
highly eulogized in several papers and periodicals,
and many flattering testimonials have I received
from private friends. I shall only quote one sen-
tence from a popular newspaper :—" It is one of
the simplest, ripest, and most spiritual expositions
of the last, and noblest, and most comprehensive
of all the messages of God. . . . . The Lectures
reflect credit at once on the head and heart
of the author." *

* During a visit to Edinburgh in 1858, I had the pleasure

Subsequently, in the Chapel, I delivered Lectures on the History of the Israelites, from the earliest times to the reign of Hezekiah. But none of them were committed to writing.

I may here add that, in 1867, at the instigation of my old friend, Mr. Benham, I wrote an " Essay on the Educational Uses of the Proverbs of Solomon." Of this, nearly 8,000 copies were distributed. It was highly appreciated in many quarters. *Proverbs.*

In 1873, *Mr. Benham* died, in his 85th year. I had been intimate with him for fifty years, and assisted him very *extensively* in the compilation and writing of his various essays, &c. But for this work, and other similar labours, the only recompense I received was the pleasure of having done it. Mr. Benham left behind him an only daughter. He had formed a splendid library, and died worth £60,000 ! *Mr. Benham.*

In May, 1855, my beloved and venerable father departed this life, in his 83rd year. He was highly respected by all who knew him, and distinguished by masculine common sense and a clear judgment—endowed with *Father's death.*

of presenting a copy of my *Lectures* to the Rev. John Brown, grandson of the well-known author of the " *Dictionary of the Bible.*" He was very cordial, and made many inquiries about the Moravian Brethren. On parting, he gave me a copy of his Sermons. Within a few months after my visit he died, at a very advanced age.

a spirit of indomitable perseverance, and a contempt for all that was mean, sordid, and frivolous. In cases of distress and difficulty his advice was eagerly sought and highly valued. He was contented with his own position in life, but rejoiced that his sons had profited by the education he had been able to bestow upon them. They had also profited largely by his admonitions, his example, and his prayers. With him Religion was a living principle, not a lifeless profession. Nevertheless, he was not perfect. His temper was occasionally quick and hasty—especially when he came in contact with laziness, indifference, and selfishness—

" The best of men have dross mixed with the gold."

His four sons in London, and two grandsons,
Funeral. went down to the funeral. There was a great gathering around the grave. The aged and grey-headed of his own and the neighbouring villages were there—the young men joined with their elders ; and many of the higher classes drew nigh, to show their respect for departed worth and their sympathy with sorrowing relatives.

Did we sorrow ? Did we not rather rejoice that our beloved father had been spared to us so long —that his illness had been brief—that his dying moments were peaceful—that he had departed without suffering—his soul filled with the hope of a glorious immortality !

On this occasion, we received many kind invitations from various quarters. In particular, I made the acquaintance and enjoyed the hospitality of Professor Cairns, Mr. Ramsay, Mayor of Berwick, Mr. Home, the Town Clerk, and the brother of Dr. Lee, of Edinburgh.

My seventh son, *Samuel*, who went with us to his grandfather's funeral, was then in his sixteenth year. Failing eyesight compelled him to abandon the printing. In 1860 he went to Ceylon, to carry on a photographic business which had been purchased by his brother William. He was soon, however, prostrated by fever, and obliged to leave the island. On his return, he was shipwrecked on the French coast, near Boulogne, and lost most of his luggage. He reached home in shattered health; but, under his mother's careful nursing, he soon recovered. He found employment as a teacher in a school in the North of *Ireland*, and, afterwards, in the same capacity, at Mirfield, in Yorkshire. Here his gifts as a public speaker were developed, and eventually (having being married in 1866) he was sent as a Moravian Missionary to Barbados, in the West Indies. In a few months he was compelled to return by a violent attack of fever. He and his wife went to *Dublin*, where he established a boarding-school, which has proved eminently successful.*

In 1868 his mother and I visited him, travelling

* In 1869 he was ordained by the Bishop of Down.

by way of Bangor and Holyhead. We were much impressed with the grandeur of the Welsh scenery. At Dublin we spent several pleasant days, visiting Kingstown and Killiney, the Dargle and Powerscourt Waterfall, Phœnix Park, Howth Lighthouse, &c.

By the death of our venerable father the attraction which had so repeatedly drawn us to the Tweed was much weakened. Only twice since that event have I visited it. The last time was in 1869, with my brother Alexander. It was a trip to be remembered. Besides revisiting all the old familiar scenes, we went to Holy Island, and, crossed the harbour from that place in a fishing coble. We were bound for *Bamborough Castle*, but, missing the Ferry, we had to walk eight miles round an inlet of the sea. In *Bamborough Church* we found the stone which covers the grave of one of our maternal ancestors, who had held high office in the castle; and in the *churchyard* we saw the monument erected to the memory of *Grace Darling*, who, with her father, had so nobly rescued the shipwrecked crew and passengers of the *Forfarshire*. The monument is not over the grave, but more to the right, where the visitor, standing by it, commands a full view of the Farne Islands, where the vessel was wrecked. We were sorry to find that the weather had so corroded the stone as to render the inscription nearly illegible.

The *castle* stands on a high, precipitous rock. The walls are very ancient, but the buildings within are mostly modern, and kept in good order. There is a fine old library, and a collection of curiosities. There is a *well* in the interior of great depth, sunk through solid rock—a work of immense labour. There is no record to show when it was accomplished, nor even when the old castle itself was built. There are many singular *legends* about it, still current among the people. Lord Crewe, Bishop of Durham,* the last proprietor (?), devised large sums to Bamborough, for educational and eleemosynary purposes, and also for the relief of sailors wrecked on the coast. During our visit the Education Commissioners had caused much consternation by threatening to overhaul the accounts of the Trustees !

The day after our return from Bamborough we were joined by my son *Samuel* and two friends from *Ireland*. So we arranged to make a pilgrimage to *Abbotsford*. Next morning we started by rail, passing through Norham to *Kelso*, where we halted and visited the ruins of the old abbey. Not far from it stands *Fleurs Castle*, the seat of the Duke of Roxburgh. [I had previously

* Baron as well as Bishop. He purchased from Government the forfeited estates of his brother-in-law, John Forster, Esq., M.P. for Northumberland, General of the rebels in 1715. From his family I am maternally descended. The estates (including Bamborough Castle, &c.) were valued at £1,314 a year.

visited it.] Resuming our journey, we went through St. Boswell's to *Melrose*. Here we stopped, and proceeded to the celebrated ruins of the *Abbey*. After examining them, we walked to *Abbotsford*, and were shown over the house, so full of reminiscences of the gifted *Sir Walter*. I noticed in the Visitors' Book that the majority of names of recent date were American. After gratifying our curiosity we returned home. The weather was fine, and the scenery beautiful and full of interest, so that we all thoroughly enjoyed the excursion.

On the following day we took a boat up the Tweed, to the *Chain Bridge*—very pleasant to the younger members of our party. On our return in the evening, we were met by a deputation from the Chapel where my father had been an Elder for above forty years—requesting me to *preach* on the following morning (Sunday). This was short notice. But I consented without hesitation, for by experience I knew that *ideas* only were wanted—*words* would be forthcoming—" The thoughts unravel tripping o'er the tongue." So I began to think, not to write. Next morning I walked down to the Chapel, and found a large congregation assembled. The Minister wished to invest me in gown and bands, but I objected. I conducted the whole Service, including a discourse which lasted forty minutes. I had not a line of notes—

Preach at Spittal.

yet (with God's help) I never faltered for a word, but spoke with force and freedom. When the heart is in the work, *On Ps. xxiii.* there is no fear of failure. I have more than once been called on to speak under similar circumstances.

Before returning to London, my brother and I again visited Edinburgh, *Roslyn Chapel*, &c.

In November, 1871, we had to mourn the loss of our youngest and beloved son, *George*. He had joined the Rifle Volunteers, and in a review at Brighton (lying in ambush on the wet grass) caught a severe cold. It developed into consumption, which carried him off in his thirtieth year. He left a widow and one boy—a fine little fellow, who is now under our special care.

In the following year his brother *William* died in Ceylon. He had been sent to that island in 1849, as the Government Printer, taking with him a wife and child. He found that the Printing-office required reforming, and he presently changed Dutch deliberation into English energy. The business rapidly increased, and he requested an assistant. This he soon obtained, his younger brother, *Henry*, being sent out in 1852. But he died of fever a few months after he had landed, in his twenty-second year. Poor dear *Henry!* His special gift was music. He was a proficient on the piano ; and before he was twenty-one, was appointed *organist* of the German Chapel in the Savoy, of which Dr. Steinkopff was then minister. His early promise of usefulness was nipped in the bud !

Another assistant was speedily sent to William, and on the further increase of the Government printing, his son George was appointed as deputy. The Photographic concern was afterwards conducted by his eldest son, William. He himself had enjoyed good health in the island. But in 1864 his beloved wife was seized with fever, and died greatly lamented. In the following year he obtained twelve months' leave of absence, and returned to England with his little ones. During that period he visited many parts of England and Ireland, and gave lectures in some places on Ceylon, which were very favourably received. He had intimated an intention of delivering one of these lectures in Fetter Lane, London. But while

Lecture on Ceylon. the lecturer was still in the country, one of his friends advertised that the lecture would be delivered on a certain day. The day came, but not the man. And the gentleman who had mistaken the date called upon me, in trouble. I advised him to deliver the lecture himself ! I knew the advice was absurd. He naturally said : " Could you venture to do it, with only six hours' notice ? " " I will try," I replied. So it was arranged I should take the lecturer's place, and so prevent disappointment.

It was too late to countermand the announcement.

I went to the Office as usual, but employed one of my sons to collect a few facts; and knowing where to look for information, I obtained and digested, in the course of four hours, materials sufficient for a lecture (delivered without notes) which lasted about an hour and a half. I was highly complimented on my effort. The subject was interesting, and new to nearly all the audience; and I may be pardoned for adding that, on its conclusion, the gentleman referred to said to my son: "What a wonderful memory your father must have!" Yes—but who gave the memory?

Shortly afterwards, William married a second wife, and returned to Ceylon. The Colonial Government had previously shown their appreciation of his services by doubling his salary. He had, besides materially reducing the expenditure of the office, although the work had annually increased, edited for several years the "Ceylon Almanac," which was a Government affair;—and otherwise employed his pen extra-officially.

I have already stated that he undertook the printing of my Lectures in Ceylon. But, in 1868, he printed a work of his own—a volume of poetry—called "The *Knuckles*, or *Mountain Life* and Coffee Cultivation in Ceylon." The poetry is not first-rate, but the notes are valuable. Again, in 1870, he published a work called "*Adam's Peak*."

It contains much interesting matter connected with that celebrated mountain in Ceylon, and traditional and historical notices of the Island. He had made three excursions himself to the " Sacred Foot-Print."

His last work was printed in 1872, " *On Early Typography.*" He barely lived to see it through the Press. The first copy he at once posted to his beloved mother. Besides this, only a few copies have reached England ; four or five are in the hands of relatives. The remainder have been secured by my worthy friend, Mr. QUARITCH, the intelligent and enterprising bookseller of Piccadilly, whose splendid *Classified Catalogue* (recently published) of *Books*, in all languages, and on all subjects, with copious and interesting notes, is unrivalled in the annals of Bookselling.

The death of our beloved son was a heavy blow. His loss was felt and deplored by a large circle in Ceylon, as it was by all who had known him at home. He was distinguished by indomitable perseverance and a very retentive memory. He was a ready and fluent speaker, possessing the rare faculty of rapidly concentrating and arranging his thoughts, and uttering them in unpremeditated and appropriate language.

His illness was brief and his end peaceful. He may be said to have died in harness, and in the prime of his life—for he had only just completed his fiftieth year.

Though I had now attained to the age of *more than threescore and ten*, I was still equal to all the requirements of the Printing- *Old Age.* office, with mental faculties and eyesight unimpaired, and possessing much of my former vigour and activity. With *Mr. Norman*, however, I am sorry to say, it was otherwise; he had been constrained, by failing sight, to withdraw from the active superintendence of the business, which, for about fifty years, he had so successfully conducted. But his place has been well and worthily supplied by his son and partner (Mr. William Norman), who, with a thorough knowledge of Printing, inherits all the sterling qualities of his excellent and venerable father. From the son, as from the father, I have ever received the kindest and most respectful attention. And when, at the close of 1875, *being in my seventy-ninth year*, it became evident to myself that bodily strength was failing, they both united in a desire that I should enjoy a season of *rest*—so long as life should be prolonged. This was accompanied by the spontaneous offer of a provision for that purpose—liberal beyond my expectations. . . . Most heartily do I pray that the old proverb may be verified in their own experience : " The liberal soul shall be made fat." Their flattering expressions of acknowledgment for my long services I shall not presume to repeat—but I shall ever feel I owe them a large amount of gratitude—and to the

Almighty, unceasing thankfulness—for the goodness and mercy that have followed me all the days of my life.

During my long term of office as *overseer*, no doubt I occasionally blundered, while vigorously pressing forward the work. But my steady object was ever to do justly between master and men. With the latter I have had very few disputes—and am willing to admit that most of these arose through suffering my impatience to override my judgment. Though the laziness of some and the incapacity of others were at times very trying.

To the compositors I leave behind me in the office (especially the older hands) I have been much indebted. They could always be depended upon :—and their steadiness, ability, and intelligence were ever equal to the emergencies of business—and materially lightened my anxiety in bringing work to a satisfactory conclusion. I was also ably seconded by my eldest son *James*, who for many years has worthily occupied the onerous position of *Reader*.

The character of " Printers " has greatly improved since I first knew London. They were then spoken of as a " *drunken set*," though I verily believe they were no worse than their neighbours. The general tone of morality is, no doubt, much higher than it was about sixty years ago. Then drunkenness was indeed very prevalent :—

and the scenes I have witnessed on Sunday mornings, in front of " Thompson's " gin-shop, on Holborn Hill, would scarcely be credited now,—and Printers were to be found in the drunken mob.

The influence of the more sober and steady men, however, began to be felt :—and the establishment of coffee-shops—which now abound, but were then unknown—removed a great temptation to resort to the Public-house.

I believe the *compositors* of the present day may rank with the most steady, as they are certainly the most intelligent, class of workmen in the Metropolis.   May they ever so continue !

ROBERT SKEEN.

10, NEVIL'S COURT, FETTER LANE,
   March 10, 1876.

WYMAN AND SONS, PRINTERS, GREAT QUEEN STREET, LINCOLN'S-INN FIELDS, W.C.

ROBERT SKEEN'S

AUTOBIOGRAPHY.

www.ingramcontent.com/pod-product-compliance
Lightning Source LLC
Chambersburg PA
CBHW081525040426
42447CB00013B/3348

9 781535 800990